"*And may a blessing come upon thy wife and upon your parents. And may you see your children, and your children's children, unto the third and fourth generation: and may your seed be blessed by the God of Israel, who reigneth for ever and ever.*"
—Gabelus to Tobias
(*Tobias* 9:10-11)

*Tobias draws the fish from the water
under St. Raphael's direction.*

ST. RAPHAEL

ANGEL OF MARRIAGE, OF HEALING, OF HAPPY MEETINGS, OF JOY AND OF TRAVEL

By
Angela Carol

*"For I am the angel Raphael,
one of the seven, who stand before
the Lord."*
—Tobias 12:15

TAN BOOKS AND PUBLISHERS, INC.
Rockford, Illinois 61105

Nihil Obstat: John J. Jennings
                     Censor Librorum

Imprimatur: ✠ Clarence G. Issenmann
                     Auxiliary Bishop of Cincinnati
                     July 31, 1954

Retypeset and republished in 1999 by TAN Books and
Publishers, Inc.

Library of Congress Catalog Card No.: 99-70785

ISBN 0-89555-650-2

Cover illustration: St. Raphael, by Brother Simeon,
1986. Copyright Monastery Icons 1986, Borrego Springs,
California. Used by arrangement with Monastery Icons.
Tel.: 800-729-4952.

Printed and bound in the United States of America.

TAN BOOKS AND PUBLISHERS, INC.
P.O. Box 424
Rockford, Illinois 61105
1999

"Joy be to thee always. . . . Be of good courage, thy cure from God is at hand."

—St. Raphael
(*Tobias* 5:11-13)

CONTENTS

Introduction to St. Raphael

Of the seven angelic spirits who chant an unending hymn of praise before the throne of the Most High God, the canonical Scriptures mention three by name: these are the Archangels Michael, Gabriel and Raphael.

The Archangel Michael, whose name means literally "Who is like God?", is the leader of the heavenly hosts in the war against the spirits of darkness.

Gabriel, the "man of God" foretold to the prophet Daniel the coming of the Messias; he is the Angel of the Annunciation, who uttered the immortal *Ave!* to the Mother of Our Lord.

Raphael, whose name in Hebrew signifies "God has healed," may be regarded as the most "human" of these angels because of the special nature of his mission. Raphael is the auxiliary of Providence, the instructor, healer and comforter of mankind. He is frequently spoken of as St. Raphael, and that too is correct, for the word "Saint" comes from the Latin *sanctus* which means "holy." Angels, as well as human beings of extraordinary holiness, are called Saints. In the case of human beings, it is necessary that they be canonized by the Church. This involves a process of investigation into the life, virtues and defects of a person who has given evidence of heroic sanctity. In regard to Angels, however, Holy Scripture itself tells us about their heavenly glory.

It is to the Archangel Raphael that this little booklet will introduce you, so that he might help and comfort you, even as he has aided countless thousands of others whose prayers he has presented to the Divine Omnipotence.

Angels: A Truth of Faith

Some people who otherwise have a great devotion to Saints may find it difficult to believe that Angels really do exist, because one does not ordinarily see, touch or hear an Angel, and of course, there are no relics that one can venerate, as in the case of human Saints. Perhaps it has become all too customary to think of Angels merely as ornaments of religious and sometimes profane art, or as poetic embellishments of sentimental songs. Perhaps we get into the habit of underestimating their powers, forgetting that there is a spiritual world, just as real as the material world that is so familiar to our senses.

Angels are spiritual beings endowed with intelligence, free will and great power. They were created by God to know, love and serve Him in Heaven. Angels are messengers sent by God—who is Himself a spirit—to the world inhabited by men. They also act as guardians of mankind.

The Scriptures tell us there are nine choirs of angels: Seraphim, Cherubim, Thrones, Dominations (which, according to some theologians, are the "assisting Angels" at God's throne), Principalities, Powers, Virtues, Archangels and Angels (described as "administering Angels" because they minister to material creation).

God may use Angels, like other creatures, in working miracles. Good Angels can inspire men to do the will of God and practice virtue. Bad angels (the devils), those who were cast from Heaven after their rebellion, can wage spiritual warfare upon mankind by means of temptation.

Angels sometimes assume bodies in order

to carry out God's commands. In this way they become perceptible to the human senses. It was thus in bodily form that the three Angels appeared to Abraham outside his tent, yet he intuitively knew they were messengers of the Lord. It was an Angel in man's form who struggled with Jacob and gave him the name "Israel." And also in many other portions of the Scriptures we find Angels appearing in the guise of men. So, according to the Biblical account, did Raphael appear to Tobias and his son.

Devotion to St. Raphael

Although St. Raphael is not mentioned by name in the New Testament, many commentators, basing their conjectures on the healing significance of his name, identify him with the "Angel of the Lord" mentioned in John 5:4, who descended at certain times into the pool called *Probatica* (or in Hebrew, *Bethsaida*) to stir the healing waters therein. In fact, bearing out that tradition, this is the Gospel read at the Mass for the Feast of St. Raphael, which the traditional calendar of the Church celebrates on October 24th.

Devotion to St. Raphael has been handed down through the ages, and churches and shrines have been erected in his honor throughout the world. Many religious communities have placed themselves under his protection.

Devotion to our Archangel was no doubt brought to America by Spanish Franciscan missionaries. In the 1800's a group of German Catholic immigrants to the United States appropriately chose him as their guide and protector, banding themselves together as the St. Raphael Society. But it was probably not until the 1920's that the devotion began to flourish and spread in this country, due to the zeal of Sister Mary Jerome, I.H.M.

One day, in her convent at Monroe, Michigan, Sister Mary Jerome happened to be looking for a Latin book when she came upon an essay on the "Holy Angels" by the French writer, Ernest Hello. She was impressed by his prayer to the Archangel Raphael—a prayer which has since become popularly known as the "Angel of Happy Meetings Prayer" (see page 52)—and it inspired her to spread the devotion to St. Raphael.

Before her death in 1952, Sister Mary
Jerome had received thousands of proofs of
the power of his intercession. Others—
among them Serena Ward, who for many
years conducted the "Whisperings" column
in a popular Catholic magazine—have car-
ried on the work of making the Archangel
Raphael better known and loved. That is
also the aspiration of the present writer.

Tobias

Some seven hundred years before the
birth of our Blessed Saviour, there lived a
very virtuous man named Tobias. He was a
true Israelite, of the tribe and city of Neph-
tali, which was in Galilee. He had an only
son who was also called by the same name,
Tobias. They lived during the time of the
Jews' captivity under the Assyrian King
Salmanasar, in the city of Nineve. The full
account of their meeting with the Archangel
Raphael can be found in the Holy Bible
(Book of *Tobias* or *Tobit*), but, briefly, it is
this:

One day Tobias the elder, due to a strange
accident, became totally blind. Because of
this sudden affliction, his family became

very poor, so that even his wife Anna had to go out to work as a weaver. Nevertheless, Tobias (whose name means "Yahweh is good") remained constant in his prayers, begging God very fervently to have mercy on him and his wife and son. Although many of his fellow Israelites laughed and mocked him for this, Tobias continued steadfast in his faith and hope.

At the same time, in the city of Rages, which was in Media, there lived a man named Raguel, a kinsman of Tobias. He had an only daughter, Sara. This young woman was very unhappy because seven times she had been given in marriage, and each of her husbands in turn had been killed by an evil spirit on their wedding night. To add to this misery, a servant maliciously accused Sara of having murdered them. However, despite all she suffered in her heart, Sara continued to pray to God with tears and fasting. And in God's inscrutable wisdom, her prayers would be answered simultaneously with the prayers of the elder Tobias. The Bible states, ". . . the holy angel of the Lord, Raphael, was sent to heal them both." (*Tob.* 3:25).

Old Tobias did not know that this wonderful thing was about to happen. Thinking, instead, he would soon die, he called his son, counselled him wisely in the love of God and neighbor, and told him to prepare for a journey to collect a just debt that had been owed to him for many years by a man named Gabelus, in the same city where Sara lived.

Young Tobias was perplexed. He had no idea how to reach that distant city, nor how he would be able to collect the debt from a man he did not even know. However, he decided to follow his father's advice and overcome his difficulty by selecting a guide for the journey. Just as he went out to seek one, he noticed a handsome young man, attired as though for travel, standing outside their house. He did not know this was an Angel of God. Nevertheless, he spoke courteously to the young man, and they arranged to go together on this long trip. Before leaving, Tobias brought the young stranger to meet his blind father. The Archangel Raphael (for that is who it was), upon entering the house, greeted old Tobias, saying, "Joy be to thee always . . . Be of good courage, thy cure from God is at hand." (*Tob.* 5:11-13).

When old Tobias wanted to know his name, St. Raphael replied evasively that he was Azarias, son of the great Ananias. He must have been smiling when he said this, for although he could not yet disclose to them his true name, he gave them a real clue to his identity: *Azarias*, in Hebrew, signifies "help of God," while *Ananias* means "grace of God"—and this was precisely the substance of the Angel's mission on earth: to teach mankind that our *"help from God"* depends on our being in *God's grace.*

Blind Tobias, when his wife Anna began to lament their son's departure, comforted her, saying, "I believe that the good Angel of God doth accompany him and doth order all things well that are done about him, so that he shall return to us with joy." (*Tob.* 5:27) Little did he realize then how true his words were!

The Journey of Tobias

With his father's blessing, young Tobias started out on this journey, accompanied by the Angel. The Bible account also mentions that Tobias' faithful little dog followed them.

When they came to the river Tigris, which formed a boundary between ancient Assyria and the land of the Medes, they were confronted by a huge, man-eating fish that would have attacked Tobias, but the Angel Raphael told him how to overcome it. After they had caught the monstrous fish, Raphael instructed Tobias to keep certain parts of it—the heart, gall and liver—to use as medicines and for driving out evil spirits. (These things, of course, had no power in themselves—it simply pleased God to show His power through them.)

When they arrived at last in the city of Rages, the Angel straightway guided Tobias to the house of Raguel because, as he explained, they were of the same tribe and distantly related to each other. Furthermore, the Angel Raphael disclosed to Tobias that Raguel's daughter, Sara, was to become his bride. This announcement frightened Tobias because he had already heard what had happened to the other seven who had married her. However, the Angel explained that all the others had been struck dead for their sins, because they had not regarded marriage as holy, but as something to serve their evil passions. Now, Tobias was to take

Sara as his wife for love of God and posterity—children—and for that reason their
marriage would be blessed and happy.

Sara's father joyfully welcomed Tobias
under his hospitable roof and consented to
the marriage when he also was assured by
the Angel that there was nothing to fear
this time, because God had kept Sara safe
for the very purpose that she might be married to such a God-fearing young man as
Tobias.

On his wedding night, Tobias burned part
of the liver of the fish (as he had been told
to do), and in that same moment the Angel
Raphael bound up the demon Asmodeus,
who had caused the death of Sara's previ-
ous bridegrooms.

Tobias and Sara spent three days and
nights in prayer before consummating their
marriage. "For," as Tobias said to his bride,
"we are the children of saints, and we must
not be joined together like heathens that
know not God." (*Tob.* 8:5). Therefore, they
first gave praise and blessing to God, and
then asked Him for health, and for posterity
in which His name might be glorified forever, and for a long life together.

The Angel Raphael, meanwhile, went to

invite Gabelus to the wedding feast which, according to ancient Jewish custom, lasted a week or longer. Overjoyed at meeting the son of his old friend and benefactor, Gabelus gladly repaid the debt he owed, thus permitting Tobias to give to Sara's parents the customary *mohar*, or marriage present.

Tobias' Return

After the nuptial festivities were over, Tobias and his bride Sara, and the servants and beasts and other goods she had received as her marriage dowry, returned to his father's house with the Angel Raphael.

In those days, a journey of this kind took many months, and during young Tobias' long absence his parents, naturally, were worried and anxious about him. However, their tears and loneliness were instantly turned to joy when they heard the barking of the faithful little dog, which, running ahead of the caravan, came wagging his tail gleefully, as though he knew he was bringing good news.

Young Tobias, entering the house, first gave thanks to God. After that, he kissed his parents and anointed his father's eyes with the gall of the fish, as the Angel had told him to do. Thereupon the elder Tobias immediately regained his sight, and they all glorified and adored God.

They also wanted to thank the young stranger who had been Tobias' friend and guide on the journey, not knowing yet that it was an Angel sent from God who had dispensed these blessings to them. In the fullness of their joy, they called him and asked him to take half of all their possessions. To this, however, the Angel replied:

"Bless ye the God of heaven, give glory to Him in the sight of all that live, because He hath shown His mercy to you . . ." And addressing the elder Tobias in particular, he continued, "When thou didst pray with tears . . . I offered thy prayer to the Lord. And because thou wast acceptable to God, it was necessary that temptation should prove thee. And now the Lord hath sent me to heal thee and to deliver Sara, thy son's wife, from the devil. For I am the Angel Raphael, one of the seven, who stand before the Lord."

Then the Bible narrative continues:

"And when they had heard these things, they were troubled, and being seized with fear they fell upon the ground on their face.

"And the Angel said to them: 'Peace be to you; fear not. For when I was with you, I was there by the will of God: bless ye Him and sing praises to Him. I seemed indeed to eat and to drink with you: but I use an invisible meat and drink which cannot be seen by men. It is time therefore that I return to Him that sent me. But bless ye God, and publish all His wonderful works.'

"And when he had said these things, he was taken from their sight, and they could see him no more. Then they, lying prostrate for three hours upon their face, blessed God: and rising up, they told all His wonderful works." (*Tob.* 12:6-22).

Because of the particular miracles he obtained for Tobias and his family, St. Raphael is universally regarded as the patron of happy and holy marriage, and also as patron of travelers, the sick and those in financial distress. Because of his role as healer, he is sometimes called the "Physician of God" or the "Medicine of God."

Angel of Health

The Angel Raphael's mission to Tobias and his family was not only to bring them the joy of spiritual blessings, but also to effect the cure of a physical affliction. The Bible tells us distinctly, "The holy Angel of the Lord, Raphael, was sent to heal them. . . ." (*Tob.* 3:25).

The problem of pain and suffering has been a mystery throughout the ages. Only too often, bodily ailments have been regarded with fear and accepted reluctantly as a harsh, though necessary punishment for sin. They should rather be looked upon as blessings in disguise, as a means to draw us closer to God and an occasion for proving our love for Him. Had the elder Tobias become sullen and resentful of the blindness that befell him, it is possible that God would not have shown him any special mercy. However, Tobias did not blaspheme because of his affliction; rather, he "continued immovable in the fear of God, giving thanks to God all the days of his life." (*Tob.* 2:14). That is an important lesson to remember.

Many of us, grieving over a sudden mis-

fortune, will moan: "Why has this happened
to me? Why does God punish me? What
have I done to deserve such a cross?" Tobias,
however, bore his affliction patiently and
blessed God for it. Consequently, he gained
much by this seemingly unfortunate expe-
rience, for there is no misfortune that God
cannot turn into a blessing for those who
love Him.

God has the right to intervene by supernatural means of His own choosing, and it
is not for us to dictate to Him how and when
this should be done. When a situation
becomes extreme, because of man's folly or
helplessness, the action of God's omnipotence shines forth more clearly. Furthermore, while waiting for a sign of divine
mercy, man has the chance to practice the
virtues of patience, humility and faith. Let
us not be hasty in our judgments, lest we
fail to see the good in what seems to be bad
fortune.

The Angel Raphael did not cure Tobias
at once, nor did he effect the cure by saying some potently mysterious words over
him. Rather, the Angel instructed Tobias'
son to make use of purely natural means—
creating a remedy compounded from God-

given things. Our Lord Himself, it will be remembered, also frequently used simple and natural things, such as clay and spittle, in performing miraculous cures. These natural objects had no magic properties of their own (though they may be symbolic of mysteries too profound for us to understand), but it was God's power working through them that effected the cure. (In our own day we have the "wonder drugs" which some people might have regarded as miraculous not so very long ago. They are not miraculous in the strict sense of the word, but they have been provided for us by God who left it to man to discover their use.)

Now, it is good Catholic teaching that if we are sick, or want to ward off illness, we should make use of the remedies that God has put into the hands of those whose lives are dedicated to a study of medicine and healing. However, when natural means are exhausted and no relief is obtained, we may ask God prayerfully for a miracle of healing as a sign of His special mercy toward us.

To Obtain God's Mercy

Did the elder Tobias do anything to deserve God's special mercy? The Bible gives us a long account of the many acts of charity that Tobias had performed; it also speaks of his intense love of God, his generosity, wisdom and kindness. See even how his old debtor, Gabelus, speaks of him upon meeting his son: "The God of Israel bless thee, because thou art the son of a very good and just man, and that feareth God, and doth almsdeeds. . . ."(*Tob.* 9:9). Tobias' goodness must have been really remarkable if a man who had not seen him for many years could still remember it so vividly. In fact, Tobias was a veritable Saint, one of the holy persons of the Old Testament. And because he bore his affliction so patiently and humbly, God responded with abundant loving-kindness and mercy.

But what about those who are not virtuous and holy? Can they hope for special favors? God's mercy is great, even to a sinner, and if the sinner is willing to amend his ways, God will not turn a deaf ear to his entreaties. However, if one feels that because of his sins he is unworthy to approach God directly, he can confidently place his cause in the hands of the Blessed Virgin or any of the Saints, who will plead for him before the throne of Almighty God. Since Biblical times, Raphael, the "heavenly physician," has obtained miracles of healing for many people in all walks and states of life who piously commended themselves to him.

Be of Good Courage

Be of good courage! That is another lesson that Saint Raphael wants to instill in our minds. Too often when we are touched by some misfortune, we become despondent and lose hope. Thereby we lose whatever chance we might have had of obtaining a supernatural cure for our afflictions. Notice how the Angel Raphael greeted the blind Tobias: "Be of good courage; thy cure from God is at hand." In other words: "Have the courage to believe!"

Most of us are afraid, really afraid, to believe that our prayers will be answered and "come true." That is just what the devil wants—he wants to subject us to his kind of "brain-washing," because by destroying our faith and confidence, he hurls an insult at God's omnipotence. When we pray half-heartedly (thinking, perhaps, "Well, I'm praying because I'm at the end of my rope and don't know what else I can do—but, of course, I don't expect God will answer my prayers!"), the devil swells with pride, for he has managed to place his ugly shadow between us and God. It is as though he could say, "I have eclipsed the Power of the Almighty and have made men blind and foolish!"

Thy cure from God is at hand! This portion of the Angel Raphael's message to Tobias teaches us two things: One is that our help is from God, and God alone. Physicians of body or soul—whether Angels or Saints, priests or doctors—all are but the ministers of God's mercy, either by supernatural or by natural means. The other point of the message is that our help lies within our reach, *at hand,* for God has wisely provided all the things that we truly need, if we know how to use them or make an effort to learn about them. Prayer is one of these means—a most important one.

Angel of Love

When Sara was languishing in her lonely sorrow, she prayed to God in these beautiful words:

"For Thy counsel is not in man's power, but this everyone is sure of that worships Thee, that his life, if it be under trial, shall be crowned: and if it be under tribulation, it shall be delivered: and if it be under correction, it shall be allowed to come to Thy mercy. For Thou art not delighted in our being lost: because after a storm Thou makest a calm, and after tears and weeping, Thou pourest in joyfulness. Be Thy name, O God of Israel, blessed forever." (*Tob.* 3:20-23).

What humility and dependence Sara expresses, what confidence and hope in God's mercy! It could be compared to the childlike confidence of St. Thérèse of Lisieux—this simple, loving and boundless confidence, which is the first step in the ascent to sanctity.

If Sara had lived a self-centered and complacent existence, we probably would never have heard of her. But since God chose to

put her to a test—indeed, a sevenfold trial—
she attained heroic significance and merited a wonderful reward in her marriage to
the young Tobias. This marriage, too, would
not be held up as an example now, centuries later, to young people today, if it had
not been singularly distinguished by its holiness and sacramental purity.

So highly does the Church regard the
union of Tobias and Sara that the Introit
of the nuptial Mass is taken from the Book
of Tobias: "May the God of Israel join you
together: and may He be with you, who was
merciful to two only children: and now, O
Lord, make them bless Thee more fully."
(*Tob.* 8:18-19). The blessing also echoes the
words of Raguel, Sara's father: "May the God
of Abraham, the God of Isaac, and the God
of Jacob be with you, and may He fulfill His
blessing in you. . . ." (*Tob.* 7:15).

Thus, in a sense, the nuptials of Tobias
and Sara were a preparation for that ulti-
mate moment when Christ, at the marriage
feast in Cana of Galilee, would raise the natural marriage bond between man and
woman to the supernatural order of a Sacra-
ment. This is the sublime meaning of the
beautiful prayer that young Tobias, Sara's

chaste bridgeroom, uttered on their wedding night:

"Lord God of our fathers, may the heavens and the earth and the sea, and the fountains and the rivers, and all Thy creatures that are in them, bless Thee. Thou madest Adam of the slime of the earth and gavest him Eve for a helper. And now, Lord, Thou knowest that not for fleshly lust do I take my sister to wife, but only for the love of posterity, in which Thy name may be blessed for ever and ever." (*Tob.* 8:7-9). Tobias called Sara his sister because they were of the same tribe and distantly related. His use of the word here also might signify the purity and tenderness of the affection he felt for her.

Happiness in Marriage

Ask any young couple today why they want to get married and practically without exception the answer will be, "We want to be happy." They are right. Marriage should bring them happiness. But are they sure they know what happiness means and how to find it? If marriage is to result in happiness and contentment, it must be prepared for just as any vocation or state in life. Preparation for marriage, or any other calling in life, ought to begin in early childhood, because such preparation is part of the general training to meet one's problems in life. In particular, the cultivation of certain personality traits is important as a preparation for marriage to insure harmony and peaceful order in the family.

The first of these traits is self-control and self-sacrifice. Happiness in marriage requires that two people, two individual personalities, learn to adjust to each other. This can be achieved mainly by the constancy with which they show patience, consideration and forbearance for each other. Naturally, this means that each must deny himself and sacrifice some of his wishes. One of the biggest tragedies in married life results from the fact that one or both of the parties have not learned to respect the wishes and the rights of others. It is only through unselfish love that happiness can be hoped for in marriage.

It is equally important, as part of one's preparation for marriage, to be trained in simplicity; in other words, to know how to enjoy the simple things of life, how to be satisfied with little, and how to manage on a small income, if necessary. Financial problems are frequently a great source of trouble in married life, but the situation becomes disastrous only when the married couple does not want to or know how to live within their means. Young people with a modest income who dream about two-carat diamond rings, expensive cars and clothes and vacations, are certainly not going to find much happiness in marriage. They refuse to realize that the family budget must be made to fit the *actual* income. On the other hand, if a young couple has been trained to appreciate the simple things of life, if they have been trained to be thrifty and to enjoy work, they can safely venture into marriage, even on a modest income.

A third essential preparation for a happy marriage is training in chastity. Whatever a person's moral background may be, whether he is a Catholic, a non-Catholic or even a modern pagan, no one will deny the fact that a youth spent in moral chastity and continence is a solid foundation for a happy marriage. Conversely, a dissolute youth spent in violation of the Sixth Commandment is frequently one of the greatest causes of misery and tragedy in married life. The best, common-sense way to assure sexual health and happiness after marriage is to live purely before marriage. This is a recognized fact. Furthermore, the spiritual strength one acquires in the struggle for chastity will serve in good stead after marriage at those times when self-control and forbearance are necessary.

Marital Obedience

Saint Paul, in his Epistle to the Ephesians, gave divinely inspired advice for happiness in marriage, writing, "Let women be subject to their husbands, as to the Lord: because the husband is the head of the wife, as Christ is the head of the church. He is the saviour of his body. Therefore as the church is subject to Christ, so also let the wives be to their husbands in all things." (*Eph.* 5:22-24).

Most modern brides resent the idea of being subject or obedient to their husbands. But let them stop to consider this calmly. This idea is not "old-fashioned." Rather, it is ancient, as ancient as the very creation of the world, and God Himself is the author of it. Where there is harmony, there is law and order. The man leads, the woman follows—carrying with her, like an alabaster box of precious ointment, the secret wisdom of her heart. And a woman is truly wise who recognizes the necessity of man, as husband and father, being the head of the family. When a woman usurps a place that is not hers by right of nature, disorder and discord work havoc in that household. A man's natural reaction, if his wife will not let him exercise his prerogative of being the head of the family, is to slip out from under the yoke and let her carry both her burden and his!

Sara followed Tobias without a murmur into a strange land, far from the house of her childhood. Centuries later, the Mother of Our Lord, Mary Immaculate, set an example of obedience and humility for all wives and mothers in ages to come when she followed St. Joseph—to Bethlehem, to Egypt and again to Nazareth—without a question, without arguing or complaining, accepting the part assigned to her by the Divine Will.

Perhaps someone may quickly protest, "These men were Saints. My husband is far from being a Saint!" Obedience and submission in a wife, is not to be confused with downright slavery or servitude to an unworthy husband. For, as St. Paul said, "The husband is the head of the wife, as Christ is the head of the church." (*Eph.* 5:23). From this we are to understand that the wife obeys her husband for the sake of Christ and she obeys him only in those things that Christ approves or that Christ permits. Consequently, the husband cannot order her around just as he pleases, nor can he expect her to cater to every one of his whims and fancies. Christ would not approve of that.

Just as it is in no way humiliating for the Church to obey Christ, so also it should be in no way humiliating for the wife to obey her husband. Besides, this admonition, if borne in mind before marriage, would prevent many a young girl from rushing into an unsuitable marriage. For she would stop to consider whether the man she expects to marry actually has the qualities of character which merit her lifelong respect and obedience.

In the same Epistle, St. Paul instructs husbands to love their wives "as Christ also loved the church, and delivered himself up for it: that he might sanctify it." (*Eph.* 5:25-

26). The husband must love his wife and show the same boundless and self-sacrificing devotion for her that Christ showed for the Church, even to the extent of gladly giving up his own life for her, if need be. If the husband shows this love and lives up to his side of the contract, the wife will not have any difficulty in keeping her love and respect for him.

Marriage: A Path To Eternal Life

Happiness in marriage is something which must be earned; it does not come as a free bonus with the marriage license. It must be worked for. It must be paid for with self-sacrifice. One might visualize marriage as a pyramid—with pleasure, joy and happiness forming two of the sides, and suffering, forbearance and forgiveness forming the other two—while love is the crowning apex of it all.

Even as suffering is part of every individual life, so it is also part of the life of every family. There are times when sickness enters the home and threatens the life of one of the members. Everyone knows what pain and anguish the entire family goes through then. There are times when the family finances are low. It is then that the parents have to save and stint and deny themselves many things they would like to have, just in order to be able to secure the bare necessities for their young ones. Love demands many sacrifices. But it is also rich in blessings for those who realize the true meaning of Christian charity. They need only to turn their eyes to the crucifix on the wall in their home and remember that Christ sacrificed Himself for love of us, even unto death upon the Cross.

With this imprint of God's love upon their hearts, young couples embarking upon marriage have nothing to fear as long as they keep the Divine Commandments and the precepts of the Church. Their marriage will be blessed and joyful. It will not "go on the rocks" because it will be built upon the unshakable rock of faith and sacramental grace.

When young Tobias feared to take Sara as his wife because of what he had heard about the others who had married her, the Angel Raphael assured him: "Hear me, and I will show thee who they are over whom the devil can prevail. For they who in such manner receive matrimony as to shut out God from themselves, and from their mind, and to give themselves to their lust, as the horse and mule, which have not understanding, over them the devil hath power." (*Tob.* 6:16-17).

Thus, married couples should remember that their most beautiful and most elevating duty toward each other is to provide not only for each other's earthly welfare, but also for each other's eternal welfare. Marriage can be a means of sanctification, and it is a great joy for a married couple, as they grow older, to be able to say that they have helped each other attain everlasting happiness. Toward the end of life, the wife might say to her husband, "I want to thank you for loving me and providing so well for me in all things." And the husband could return the compliment and say, "I have to thank you for being such an understanding wife and for making our home so pleasant." But the greatest joy of all will come in Heaven, when they can say to each other, "I have you to thank for helping me gain eternal life. I am grateful to you for keeping my soul safe for God."

Man's Cooperation with God

One of the things that impresses us in the story of St. Raphael and Tobias is the Angel's extreme courtesy and willingness to help in whatever form or manner necessary. We seldom find this among ordinary human beings. Only too often, if we ask others for help, they are either too preoccupied with their own affairs to bother with us, or else they are not able to be of any really effective aid. Sometimes they might like to assist us, but they simply don't know how. Seldom does anyone do a whit more than duty demands.

But it is not so with an Angel—a being so closely associated with God Himself and so completely in tune with His Divine Spirit. Time and place present no obstacles to the purely spiritual activity of an Angel.

Had God wished it, the Angel Raphael could have obtained all the blessings and favors in a single instant, perhaps by saying a mysterious word, without the least bit of effort or cooperation on the part of either Tobias—father or son. But notice how St. Raphael helped them: Although possessing supernatural intelligence and the ability to do more than is within human means, the Angel Raphael did not do everything entirely by himself. He did not allow young Tobias to stand by as a passive spectator. Instructing him carefully, gradually, as they proceeded along the route, the Archangel disclosed to Tobias the knowledge and wisdom he could not have come by naturally. Each incident, each event became a lesson which the docile and obedient young pupil learned under the tutelage of his celestial guide.

God knows we are weak! For that reason He has provided us with so many helps to salvation. Through the Church He has given us the Sacraments as channels of grace; He also gave us the various sacramentals, indulgences and other spiritual aids. Above all, next to Himself, God gave us His Blessed Mother, and for our supplementary intercessors—the Angels and Saints.

Even though we are endowed with all these spiritual gifts and heavenly protectors, we frequently fall into the danger of becoming morally slothful. We often say, in effect, "Let God do it! Let the Saints do it for me!" We would like just to sit back and wait for miracles to happen. This is the danger that

young Tobias might have fallen into, had
not the Angel Raphael made him do his
part to achieve the desired ends. He had to
pray, to resist temptation . . . and to work!

Some people always complain, "Why don't
we get what we pray for?" First of all, the
favors they ask may not be in accordance
with God's supremely wise Will. Sometimes,
in their blindness, they pray for things that
would be injurious to their eternal salvation—and which even here on earth might
make them quite miserable. "God's ways are
not ours. . . ."

We may assume that God permitted the
Angel Raphael to work miracles for Tobias
and his son, not solely because of their
virtues, which they undoubtedly possessed,
but rather because God wished to show unto
mankind in general, through their particular example, that His mercy abides with us
and His blessings are upon those who love
and serve Him with their whole heart and
soul.

Prayer and Action

In regard to ourselves, God wishes to
awaken our love and zeal, to invite us to lift

up our eyes to Him as the source of our joy
and strength. He wants us to pray, and He
is not deaf to our prayers, as some people
seem to think. But we should not expect
miracles to happen without our co-operat-
ing with God's grace. We sometimes hear it
said, on the political level, that a good gov-
ernment does not do anything for its citi-
zens that they themselves can and should
do for themselves. On a higher plane, our
Heavenly Father also wants us to exercise
our powers of intelligence, action and voli-
tion. Not to make use of the talents He has
given us would be to despise His gifts.

There is hardly a single one among us
who is totally helpless. Even if a person cannot move a limb or raise an eyelid, as long
as he is alive and conscious, he has enough
active energy to lift his thoughts and his will
to God, who is the very source and abundant reservoir of all our strength and life.
It is only when we have done our part that
God will do the rest, making it perfect.

Sometimes our prayers may remain unan-
swered because we do not make the slight-
est attempt to merit special favors from God.
In regard to Tobias the elder, we read that
"he fed the hungry, and gave clothes to the

naked, and was careful to bury the dead, and they that were slain." (*Tob.* 1:20). So, in spirit at least, he was one of Christ's elect, even though he lived centuries before Our Lord's birth, and no doubt he was among those souls in Limbo whom Christ took up into Heaven after His Resurrection.

We should not think, however, that just by following Tobias' example, by giving alms or helping others in distress, we will be automatically entitled to special supernatural favors from the Almighty. It is our Christian duty to do all these good things. God will reward us, it is true, and He will bless us richly for even the smallest act of charity we perform in His name. But to demand of God to suspend or change the regular operations of nature for our sake, or expect Him to hand us some foolish bauble we are crying for like spoiled children, would be presumptuous.

There are definite natural laws that have been established by the Creator. No amount of imagining, for instance, that one can fly will make one fly like a bird. But an inventive genius, may devise some mechanical means of traveling through the air—as has already been done, of course. Or, the thoughts of a poet may have wings and carry him across time and space and even beyond. But no amount of imagining will make one sprout actual wings or make a new limb grow in place of a severed member, although with the aid of proper therapy a crippled person can learn to use an artificial replacement. The thing to bear in mind is that, with the proper mental and spiritual training, we can learn not only to overcome a disability but also to use it as a stepping stone to greater achievement. Many Saints and famous people became great because of some affliction or misfortune that they had to learn to conquer. This can be a cross that lifts one above mediocrity.

God tested the elder Tobias, as He did all the other heroes of sanctity throughout the ages, in order to bring out the best virtues in them. Yes, and that is why He tests us by permitting suffering and all sorts of calamities to befall us, not merely to punish us for sin, but rather to draw us away from sin—to make us better and make us realize that the spirit can be victorious over the flesh. For this life is but a novitiate for Heaven: a time of trial and perfecting.

When God indulges us with a special mir-

acle or a special blessing, it may be not
because we have merited it ourselves, but
because we have some loving and powerful
intercessor begging for us in Heaven, or on
earth, or even in Purgatory, for the Communion of Saints unites all in prayer.

The Science of Prayer

Prayers are potent! They have a power
that is frequently unsuspected. But they are
more than just a tool for getting what we
think we want. They are primarily an expres-
sion of love by an act of adoration to His
Infinite Majesty. They should express our
gratitude to Our Heavenly Father for all the
gifts we already have received. And only
then should they become an act of petition
for special favors and graces—although it
is always lawful and indeed pleasing to God
when we beg Him for the spiritual grace we
need.

Now, who can understand the "science of
prayer" if not an Angel? Under the special
patronage of the Archangel Raphael—who
is not only one of the seven spirits who stand
constantly before the heavenly throne, but
who has also shown himself to be so sym-

pathetically concerned with the trials and troubles of mankind—our prayers become as a fragrant cloud of incense, most pleasing to the Eternal God.

Angel of Joy

"Joy be to thee always" (*Tob.* 5:11), the Angel Raphael said when he greeted the elder Tobias. And as the Scriptures tell us, these words of St. Raphael were fulfilled:

"And after Tobias was restored to his sight, he lived two and forty years, and saw the children of his grandchildren. And after he had lived a hundred and two years, he was buried honourably in Ninive. For he was six and fifty years old when he lost the sight of his eyes, and sixty when he recovered it again. And the rest of his life was in joy, and with great increase of the fear of God he departed in peace . . .

"And it came to pass that after the death of his mother, Tobias [the younger] departed out of Ninive with his wife, and children, and children's children, and returned to his father-in-law and mother-in-law. And he found them in health in a good old age: and he took care of them, and he closed their eyes: and all the inheritance of Raguel's house came to him: and he saw his children's children to the fifth generation. And after he had lived ninety-nine years in the fear of the Lord, with joy they buried him. And all his kindred, and all his generation continued in good life, and in holy conversation, so that they were acceptable both to God, and to men, and to all that dwelt in the land." (*Tob.* 14:1-4, 14-17).

"And the rest of his life was in joy"—what wonderful words!

Joy at all times? Yes, even when we are most sorely tried. For, apart from the usual blessings of life that make us rejoice (and which we too often take for granted), we should also be glad when God sends us a cross to remind us of His own sufferings on Calvary. How often it is that only through some pain or grief do we turn our thoughts to God! When we are self-satisfied and pleased, we tend to forget about Him.

Above all, do not grumble or become despondent if your prayers are not answered immediately, or exactly the way you want. God may have other plans for you, infinitely better than any you dreamed of. Trust Him!

Angel of Light

If young Tobias felt perplexed at the thought of setting out on a journey to another city, how much greater might be our concern about our whole life's pilgrimage! Actually, Tobias was worried not so much about the distance to be covered or the time that would be consumed by the trip. It was rather the dangers lurking along the way that appalled him. He feared uncertainty and the unknown, just as do most of us.

The Biblical story speaks of a monstrous fish that would have devoured Tobias had not the Angel shown him how to gain control of it. We do not know what kind of fish this was. . . . it is not important to know what kind of fish it was, for its only purpose was to show us that God has the power to draw good out of evil. This was expressed in the Angel's instructions to Tobias that the heart, liver and gall of this dangerous fish be kept and used later for casting out an evil spirit and for healing purposes.

The ancients believed that the heart was the seat of spiritual or conscious life and love; that the liver denoted passion or desire; and the gall was supposed to be the symbol of a rancorous spirit. Thus, when the Angel told Tobias to burn the liver of the fish before entering the nuptial chamber, this action can be interpreted to mean that Tobias should restrain his concupiscence, sacrificing his desires in deference to God. In much the same way, we also, by immolating our inordinate affections, passions and desires, can purify our souls and make them pleasing in the sight of God. From the cure of Tobias' father's blindness through the application of the fish gall we might draw the lesson that our own spiritual blindness can be healed by removing the scales of bitterness and sullen pride from our eyes.

The course of our earthly pilgrimage in modern times is even more complicated, devious and beset with dangers than it was in ancient days. Life was simpler then. The people of the chosen race remembered their covenant with God. And when they erred or failed to observe the Ten Commandments, God sent His prophets or Angels to admonish them and set them on the right path.

"What lies hidden in the Old Testament,"

according to St. Augustine, "is made manifest in the New." Now we have infinitely more than the prophets. In an excess of Divine Love, God sent His own Son to be our Way, our Truth and our Life; a gift commemorated and renewed daily upon our altars, even to the end of time. We are also richer than the ancients because we have the complete Scripture, a gift of the Holy Spirit. We also have the Blessed Mother of God and all the Saints. We have the fulfillment of the promise; whereas they had only the hope.

One would think then, that such Divine generosity should be sufficient and more than enough to set us straight. One would think that out of sheer gratitude mankind would turn away from evil and follow the Redeemer's teaching and doctrine of life. Or, if not from gratitude, they should have at least the common sense to realize that this is the only practical way to achieve enduring happiness. But alas! the devils of pride, envy, anger and lust—and all the rest of Hell's legions—try without ceasing to spread their black wings across the horizon of man's intellect, to dig their claws deeper into man's heart and to press down his soul with the weight of their own abysmal despair. The demons of darkness hate the Light of God. They do all they can to confuse mankind and to prevent us from ever seeing the Beatific Vision.

Throughout the centuries many men have lost their way. It was not that God wanted them to be lost. He was there all the time, loving them, wanting to help them. But they believed in the illusory power and fascination of evil, rather than in the true power of the good God.

The signs along life's road are clear and unmistakable—one pointing to Heaven, the other to Hell. We have the God-given faculties of reason and a free will. We have only to ask for God's grace and to choose. And if we do not become blinded by pride and idolatrous love of self, we will make the right choice—the good though difficult road that leads to salvation. The sign pointing to eternal happiness is as clear and as starkly simple as the Cross.

We may well take to heart the words of a religious writer who says: "An Archangel is like a revelation, a divine message, living and communicative. Let us ask of all the Archangels . . . these beings of light . . .

the true light regarding the Divinity and Incarnation of Christ, regarding His glory and grace, and all spiritual things. The supernatural light is so precious in the practice of virtues . . . that the Archangels who receive this light from God want nothing else but to radiate it and to make our souls more fruitful in grace. This is their happiness: to announce to us the glory of God in the supernatural mysteries, for our instruction and to exhort us in a most intimate manner, penetrating to the depths of our souls as no human being can—no matter how learned. Let us then open our hearts to these living lights of God and let them stir up our wills to a new and expansive activity and zeal of soul." (Sh. Sauvé, SS. *L'Ange et L'Homme Intime*, p. 16).

May the Archangel Raphael, Angel of Light, guide us safely to our heavenly home!

Devotions in Honor of St. Raphael

Litany of Saint Raphael

From *Walking with St. Raphael,* by Fr. R. Lovasik, S.V.D.
(For private use only.)

Lord, have mercy on us.
Christ, have mercy on us.
Lord, have mercy on us. Christ, hear us.
Christ, graciously hear us.
God the Father of Heaven,
Have mercy on us.
God the Son, Redeemer of the world,
Have mercy on us.
God the Holy Ghost,
Have mercy on us.
Holy Trinity, one God,
Have mercy on us.
Jesus, King of Angels,
Have mercy on us.

Mary, Queen of Angels, *pray for us.*
St. Raphael the Archangel, *pray for us.*
St. Raphael, whose name means "God has
healed," *etc.*
St. Raphael, preserved with the good
Angels in God's kingdom, *etc.*

46

St. Raphael, one of the seven spirits who stand before the Most High,

St. Raphael, ministering to God in Heaven,

St. Raphael, noble and mighty messenger of God,

St. Raphael, devoted to the Holy Will of God,

St. Raphael, who offered to God the prayers of the elder Tobias,

St. Raphael, traveling-companion of the young Tobias,

St. Raphael, who guarded your friends from danger,

St. Raphael, who found a worthy wife for Tobias,

St. Raphael, who delivered Sara from the evil spirits,

St. Raphael, who healed the elder Tobias of his blindness,

St. Raphael, guide and protector on our journey through life,

St. Raphael, strong helper in time of need,

St. Raphael, conqueror of evil,

St. Raphael, guide and counsellor of young people,

St. Raphael, protector of pure souls,

St. Raphael, patron Angel of youth,

St. Raphael, Angel of joy,

St. Raphael, Angel of happy meetings,

St. Raphael, Angel of chaste courtship,

St. Raphael, Angel of those seeking a marriage partner,

St. Raphael, Angel of a happy marriage,

St. Raphael, Angel of home life,

St. Raphael, guardian of the Christian family,

St. Raphael, protector of travelers,

St. Raphael, patron of health,

St. Raphael, heavenly physician,

St. Raphael, helper of the blind,

St. Raphael, healer of the sick,

St. Raphael, patron of physicians,

St. Raphael, consoler of the afflicted,

St. Raphael, support of the dying,

St. Raphael, herald of blessings,

St. Raphael, defender of the Church,

Lamb of God, who take away the sins of the world, *Spare us, O Lord.*

Lamb of God, who take away the sins of the world, *Graciously hear us, O Lord.*

Lamb of God, who take away the sins of the world, *Have mercy on us.*

V. Pray for us, O glorious St. Raphael the Archangel,

R. *That we may be made worthy of the promises of Christ.*

Let Us Pray

O God, Who graciously gave the Archangel Raphael as a companion to Thy servant Tobias on his journey, grant us, Thy servants, that we may ever enjoy his protection and be strengthened by his help. Through Christ our Lord. Amen.

Imprimatur: ✠ John Mark Gannon, D.D., D.C.L., Bishop of Erie

Novena Prayer to St. Raphael

MOST illustrious Archangel St. Raphael, who faithfully accompanied the youth Tobias from Syria to Media, deign also to accompany me, a wretched sinner, on the dangerous journey which I am making now from Time to Eternity.

Glory be to the Father . . .

Most wise Archangel St. Raphael, who while walking beside the river Tigris preserved the youth Tobias from the peril of death, teaching him how to obtain control of the fish which threatened him, preserve my life also from the attacks of the monster which threatens to devour me.

Glory be to the Father . . .

Most compassionate Archangel St. Raphael, who, by a miracle wonderful in its simplicity restored the precious gift of sight to the blind Tobias, free my life, I beseech thee, from the blindness which afflicts and dishonors it, so that I may know things in their true aspect. Never permit me to be deceived by appearances, but help me always to walk secure in the way of the divine Commandments.

Glory be to the Father . . .

Most perfect Archangel St. Raphael, ever standing before the throne of the Most High to praise Him, to bless Him, to glorify Him and to serve Him, obtain for me the grace never to lose sight of the divine presence, so that my thoughts, my words and my works may be directed always to the glory of God and to my own sanctification.

Glory be to the Father . . .

Imprimatur: ✝Edward Mooney, D.D., Archbishop of Detroit
November 11, 1938

Prayer to St. Raphael for Busy People

Angel St. Raphael,
Fill my life
With happy meetings.
Let each one fulfill
The loving decrees
Of God's holy Will.
St. Raphael,
Humanity's protector,
Be thou my guide,
My friend and director.

Imprimatur: ✠Vincent S. Waters, D.D., Bishop of Raleigh

Prayer to St. Raphael for Help

O GLORIOUS ARCHANGEL, Saint Raphael, great prince of the heavenly court, illustrious by thy gifts of wisdom and grace, guide of travelers by land and sea, consoler of the unfortunate and refuge of sinners, I entreat thee, help me in all my needs and in all the trials of this life, as thou didst once assist the young Tobias in his journeyings. And since thou art the "physician" of God, I humbly pray thee to heal my soul of its many infirmities and my body of the ills that afflict it, if this favor be for my greater good. I ask especially for angelic purity, that I may be made fit to be the living temple of the Holy Ghost. Amen.

Prayer For Health
From the Little Office of the Holy Angels

O RAPHAEL of the glorious seven who stand before the throne of Him who lives and reigns, Angel of Health, the Lord hath filled thy hand with balm from Heaven to soothe or cure our pains. Heal or console the victims of disease, and guide our steps when doubtful of our ways.

"Angel of Happy Meetings" Prayer
Translated from the French of Ernest Hello

D EAR ST. RAPHAEL, Angel of Happy Meetings, lead us by the hand toward those we are waiting for and those who are waiting for us. May all our movements, all their movements, be guided by thy light and transfigured by thy joy.

Angel guide of Tobias, lay the request we now address to thee at the feet of Him on whose unveiled face thou art privileged to gaze. (*Mention your request.*) Lonely and weary, deeply grieved by the separation and sorrows of earth, we feel the need of calling out to thee and of pleading for the protection of thy wings so that we may not be as strangers in the province of joy.

Remember the weak, thou who art strong, whose home lies beyond the region of thunder, in a land that is always peaceful, always serene and bright with the resplendent glory of God. Amen.

Prayer to St. Raphael, Archangel

VOUCHSAFE, O Lord God, to send unto our assistance St. Raphael the Archangel, and may he who we believe stands evermore before the throne of Thy Majesty, offer unto Thee our humble petitions to be blessed by Thee. Through Christ Our Lord. Amen. (*Roman Missal*)

Pope Pius XI, on May 6, 1933, granted the following indulgences to the faithful who, at any time during the year, make a Novena in honor of St. Raphael the Archangel: an indulgence of five years on every day of the Novena; a plenary indulgence after completion of the Novena. Conditions for gaining the plenary indulgence: Confession, Communion, visit to a church or oratory, prayer according to the intentions of the Holy Father (at least one Our Father, Hail Mary, and Glory Be). For the Novena, any prayers approved by the proper ecclesiastical authority may be used.

If you have enjoyed this book, consider making your next selection from among the following . . .

Prices subject to change.

Prices subject to change.

Prices subject to change.